T0381121

We the People

(WTP)

COPING WITH THE CANGING TIMES

Serendipity

BALBOA.PRESS

A DIVISION OF HAY HOUSE

Balboa Press books may be ordered through booksellers or by contacting:

Balboa Press
A Division of Hay House
1663 Liberty Drive
Bloomington, IN 47403
www.balboapress.com
844-682-1282

Because of the dynamic nature of the Internet, any web addresses or
links contained in this book may have changed since publication and
may no longer be valid. The views expressed in this work are solely those
of the author and do not necessarily reflect the views of the publisher,
and the publisher hereby disclaims any responsibility for them.

The author of this book does not dispense medical advice or prescribe the use
of any technique as a form of treatment for physical, emotional, or medical
problems without the advice of a physician, either directly or indirectly. The
intent of the author is only to offer information of a general nature to help
you in your quest for emotional and spiritual well-being. In the event you use
any of the information in this book for yourself, which is your constitutional
right, the author and the publisher assume no responsibility for your actions.

Any people depicted in stock imagery provided by Getty Images are
models, and such images are being used for illustrative purposes only.
Certain stock imagery © Getty Images.

Print information available on the last page.

ISBN: 979-8-7652-5169-0 (sc)
ISBN: 979-8-7652-5170-6 (hc)
ISBN: 979-8-7652-5168-3 (e)

Library of Congress Control Number: 2024909883

Balboa Press rev. date: 06/28/2024

Contents

Introduction

Well, here we go again. For those who do not yet know about the first two books, let us do a short introduction. *Confessions from the Closet* was my first book. In all, it took thirty years to complete. The story tells what it is like to be born with psychic abilities. The world was not yet ready to hear about the subject, as I was punished for speaking of such things. I created an imaginary closet to keep all the wonderful things being psychic can be. I loved my closet. I loved the things I could do. My Old Man—that is the name given to him by the three-year-old who first spoke of him. He was my imaginary friend and grew into a guide, a guard, and a teacher.

The second book was *100 Lessons from the Closet*. I was sent away to school when I needed help overcoming a big problem. I went to school nightly to a school in my dreams. My daughter was raped. I wanted to hurt the person who did it, and I was taught healing. I wanted vengeance and was taught peace. I wanted to kill the person and was taught how to live.

I did not think it was possible for me to write a second book. I am much older now and not in good health (COVID). The second book took less than a month to write. The years between the first and the second book were filled with my apprenticeships for becoming a member of the team. The team (my teachers and I) started this third book. It is now time for the teachers and I to speak out again. We the People (WTP) need coping skills to make the best of changing times.

This third book will be nothing like what I thought it would be. I wanted to write chapters and verses about why the old school was wrong. I wanted to show how wonderful spirituality is and that being woke is really the answer. The team had other ideas. The notes of the outline showed a different way of looking at things. I will join the team and get to work. The team cuts to the chase. Other channeled books carry on and on. Other channeled books are not grounded by someone who calls Earth home. I will still give my solo input at the end of each lesson. I will address the reader directly and ask for their input. And so, it begins.

PART I

We The People (WTP)

Such Excitement

My team has gone into overdrive with the excitement of WTP. The team sent each session with fireworks. It is like the Fourth of July, setting the stage for freedom. The people who will make a difference in the new era are a force to be reckoned with. We can see the wonderful examples of WTP. On January 6, the country was saved by WTP. In times gone by, WTP were grateful to the soldiers who saved the country. The new soldiers are WTP. Everyone who stood up for the country is a member of WTP.

We can see that people make a difference. There are many heroes to thank. Each of the Capitol police officers fought to keep the insurrectionists from overtaking the country. I thank them for their service.

There is another member of WTP who needs to be thanked for his service that day. Vice President Pence was another hero. VP Pence withstood the begging from Dirty Donald and others to join the insurrectionists.

Once again, this book is not to be read as a novel. It's necessary to stop and think about the book. Stopping and talking with others will clarify things for you as well. Space is provided to keep track of your thoughts.

_____

_____

Pirates Start the Concept of WTP

The new era of WTP started with the pirates of the Caribbean. The pirates of each ship could vote for a captain. The captain would then become the leader. The leader had responsibilities to the crew. He would plan the attacks, make sure the ship was in good order, and feed and take care of the crew. The most important task of the captain was to split the bounty from the attacks. If the captain was not doing a good job, WTP (We the Pirates) could vote for a new captain. A new era had started. The idea of WTP had infected the New World. Up to that point, the station of the leader had been inherited or claimed.

Wow, surprising people brought about a new way. They had a good idea because they were not stuck or loyal to the old way of thinking. The pirates had the important ingredient of freedom.

The USA is known as the land of the free. We can vote to get the captain too. Vote. Think about which captain would keep democracy strong. What captain would keep the USA the land of the free.

_____

_____

New World / New Era

The idea of voting for a leader grew in this new land. A new age had dawned, and the story of the USA started. The rebellious nature of the pirates showed up in the newly formed territories of England and Spain and France. War in the new land was not fought for new territories. The war was fought for freedom.

The experiment of a new way of government was exciting. It was also such a dangerous time. Would you be willing to stand up for the county, even in the face of danger? I think so. Americans have always put up a good fight when needed. When it was not needed, we were just a peaceful people.

_____

_____

The Birth of Our Nation

The roots of WTP started with the grand experiment. The United States of America was born. The USA started a new type of country. The USA is a republic. It is a mistake to think that this means we are not to be ruled by a monarchy. It really means that the people will rule the country.

The roots of WTP are now reminding us of how each of us can make a difference. The new age, caused by COVID-19, climate change, and creeps will force the new era. WTP provide the unity to cope with all the changes. Evil can triumph only if good people do nothing. It is now time for WTP to show our strength.

Feel the surge of WTP. It is strong in this one. There is a Star Wars connection.

_____

_____

Vote

The way people rule is with a free and fair election. Not all countries have a free and fair election. January 6 was the first time the fairness of an election was questioned in the USA. Dirty Donald lost.

I do call him Dirty Donald. He thought he was so clever and smart by avoiding paying taxes. He was not smart; he was playing dirty. Dirty Donald then filed more than sixty lawsuits to support his imaginary claim that the election was rigged. Only one was found to have been valid. All the other lawsuits were found to be groundless.

WTP stood up again. The judges need to be thought of as heroes in the fight to keep our country strong. In these case findings, the heroes were the judges who stood for the law. Some of the judges I see now are only standing for the old ways. They have not yet realized that the country has already changed. America is already great.

My first instinct was to say how the old-school way of thinking was wrong. The response of fighting and rebelling is not the best answer. Telling them all off is not the answer either. The answer? Like in school, the first teacher was George. George made me calm enough so I could think. Meeting the new challenges and figuring out what to do is a better answer. Let it be. I have learned and understand more now. Pointing the judgment finger does no good.

I am in personal trials now. The team has started a new thing with me. They will point a finger at me when I start to fall back into the old way of condemning a person or action. When I slip, I delete it. When I get close, I think about deleting it. Getting used to the new era's ways (spirituality and wokeness) takes time. I am not quite there yet.

Yes, change is done step by step. I am still working on it. I must practice what they teach.

Cusp of a New Age

This time, the changes are bigger. The reasons for change are more numerous. The stakes are higher. We are at the edge of a new age.

Everything around you is in a state of flux. There is no place for firm footing. We have all noticed this. It is like a tennis game. We look to the left and the right, and each is stating their case. There is a war declared by the right (old school) on the left (woke). Which side are you on? Which side will win? If you know the story of the two fighting wolves, the one that wins is the one you feed.

I personally feel better now with the intent to change the way I do things. No more fighting and telling them they are wrong. I will only stand my ground. The new age will need people working at their highest level. Things will be changing.

_____

_____

Causes of the New Age: COVID-19, Climate Change, and Creeps (CCC)

WTP can handle many things. History has shown us that when times are tough, we work together and get through it. This time is a little different. There are three things that are facing us at once. Three things are shaking up the world as we know it. First came climate change. The earth itself is changing. Then came COVID-19. People were grounded in their homes. Finding a cure took time. The numbers of deaths broke up many families. Things changed. Because of these changes, some people resisted the masks and started to rebel. Even climate change was denied and fought over. The old-school way of not facing a problem and fighting instead is at the root of rebellion. Those who act out are the creeps.

What are we to do? We are to do our best.

_____

_____

Long Labor Pains

The new era will not come in the twinkling of the eye. The lead-up will take years. This gives us plenty of time to plan and deal with each problem as it comes. Each of the three Cs will come again and again in smaller measures. We are not done with COVID-19 yet. We are only starting to see the effects of climate change. The creeps are another matter. There have always been creeps, but they were once easy to handle. Now the creeps are so blatant that they can no longer be ignored. These people want to be creeps. They truly believe that only the old-school way of being and thinking is how the world must be. They have not yet realized that the new era is already here. The old school has declared war against the woke. I would rather be woke than old-school.

This is a free country. We all have free will. I was denied my freedom too many times to remain silent now.

Shout Out to WTP

We the People (WTP) stand up against bullies. WTP do not like bullies. The first time we saw bullies was in grade school. Bullies are grade-school people. WTP do not like being called names; that is grade-school stuff. Sadly, some of us never grew up.

In high school, bullies were still there. Some people never learn to get along with others. Sadly, some of us want to go back to the good old days of high school. Those people never took the next step in maturing.

In the adult world, bullies are known as narcissists. We can see how narcissists never grow up. The narcissists do not want the good old days back; they just want their way. Dirty Donald does not want to make America great again. He wants to make himself great again. Spiritually, he never got to the fourth chakra (love), so he only thinks of himself.

Time to acknowledge another WTP hero. John McCain stood up against the bully. John was someone who remained faithful to himself, his faith, and his country.

There are so many heroes with stories to tell. God bless them.

Can we add more to the list of heroes?

More Changes to Come

Now to the things that will be different in the future. Religions are going to fade away. More on this later. Maps will have to be redrawn. More on this later. Many say that it is what it is, but it really was not what it was. UFOs were covered up so that the world would not change. More on this later. The new age is so much bigger than a new era.

Chamberlain and even Kennedy spoke of living in interesting times. It is said the idea started in the seventeenth century. I must admit it is exciting to live in these times.

In the second book, I told you there would be a test. The time we are living in is the test. Use the lessons from the second book to step up to be your best self.

_____

_____

Times Have Changed

The changing times will change us.

Will you join WTP or backslide?

_____

_____

PART II

Earth Changes

Earth Changes

We have been through new ages before. History has shown us this. Before we were able to record history, the earth changed so much that those living, both human and animal, were devastated. The causes were different, but the effects were the same. The earth changed so much that those who were here were no longer able to record their history.

We can find out about things long ago through science. I love science. The different sciences contribute so much to our understanding of the history of the earth. Five to six million years ago, the Grand Canyon was formed. My husband and I visited the Grand Canyon. It is impossible to imagine its size and beauty unless you see it for yourself. I was overwhelmed.

Let that sink in. Millions of years ago. Millions of years is an unthinkable amount of time. I can see why the Christians do not like science. The findings of science negate their adherence to their Bible. Creating the world in seven days could not be understood by people of that time. More on this later.

_____

_____

Climate Changes

Science has contributed in other ways. Being forewarned is being forearmed. Science tried to tell us earlier that climate change would bring devastation to the planet. We are being shown almost daily now that the climate is changing. There is no longer any denying it. There is still time to build plans to deal with the changes. There is no stopping the process now.

The good news is that the process will take time. It will be years until we see the water take over the lands we live on. For now, the weather is the most important thing to deal with. The patterns have changed. The strength of the storms has increased. Building better and stronger is part of the answer. Moving to safer areas is another coping mechanism. Ignoring the changes is not going to help. Many will continue to be in denial, as they were while climate change was approaching, never accepting what was happening. We can no longer listen to the naysayers. Action is required. For better or worse, the new age has started.

There will be a domino effect from the changes. One thing will affect another. The temperature difference will affect the growing of food. "Deal with it" is the answer from the team. Do not take this too lightly. Making plans will allow those living on this planet to do a better job of surviving what is to come.

Many years ago, my team showed me loops of time. Time does repeat itself. The loops will keep spinning. There are, however, bigger loops. The bigger loops bring in a new age, not just a new era.

Deep Changes

It is not yet time for the other changes. It will take years for the changes to sink in. By sinking in, we mean that the deeper parts of the earth will change too. Water is the most destructive force on this planet. The water that is raining in California can erode the fault lines. It will take years, but moving is still an option. Denial is not an option. I do not want to make people panic. There will be shaking before the fall. There is time to deal with all the changes that are coming.

The deep changes will eventually sink into the very heart of the planet. The changes in the land will eventually change where the volcanoes will find their release. Again, do not panic. Years and years will give us time to harden our defenses. Years and years will help us come to our senses. WTP will need to work together worldwide to have the best outcome from the devastation that is coming. It is said that hard times bring out the best in people. I know this is true. WTP can do this.

What can be said at this point? Thinking about this and talking to others about this will help. I do admit, once again, that it is exciting to be living in these times.

_____

_____

PART III

Fed Up

PART III

Fed Up

WTP Are Fed Up

As I was writing this book, there was another shooting. This one was in Kansas City. WTP had heroes who stood up and kept track of a few shooters, and other WTPs tackled them. Thank you, once again, WTP heroes.

WTP are fed up and are now ready to stand up. On January 6, this country could not imagine that such an attack was possible. This country has seen so many discontented criminals shooting people, with or without a political statement in mind. Even now, Dirty Donald hints at what could happen when he faces the music for his crimes. WTP are now fed up and ready to stand up.

This shootout was between two different groups. There are just too many high-powered guns. I am a gun owner. I believe in protection. I do not believe in aggression. It is time for WTP to stand up and be counted to get rid of the NRA.

In my school in the sky, another lesson was balance. Never become an extremist who forces your views on everyone. I have spent a great deal of energy being in the middle. From there, I can acknowledge the rights of others. WTP work hard to bring people back to the middle. Bullies may try to push their agenda, to force others on the teeter-totter to the dangerous upper seat, knowing that they can cause harm by jumping off. The balance, where both are equal, is what WTP are seeking.

Loyalty or Betrayal

Decisions must be made by each of us because things are in such a flux. There comes a point when remaining loyal makes you betray yourself. Loyalty to a narcissist makes you betray your country. I know about this personally. I have had more than my share of dealing with narcissists. Three different narcissists are family members. I finally learned the lesson.

I wanted to hold off on writing about spirituality. Learning a lesson is part of spirituality. If at first you do not learn, you will face the same challenge again. If you are stuck on stupid, you will see the test again.

_____

_____

Tools of the Trade

A narcissist's tools of the trade are drama and lies. The drama will bring in enablers who want to help. Drama is often covered with lies. I personally have supported a narcissist for years. I wanted to stand by my sister. Then there was a step too far, and I cut her out of my life. It was not easy to do this.

Another narcissist came in the form of an in-law. I learned to just cut them off. I loved my husband, and he stood by me. The lies persisted until our marriage ended after forty-two years, when cancer took my love from me.

Narcissists will never change. With my third narcissist, I confronted him about the lies. A narcissist will never admit they lie. In the showdown with my third narcissist, he said the lies justify the means. His lies got him what he wanted. I just walked away.

The narcissist will then look for more suckers who will believe them.

I told you this story so that you do not have to fall for the lies as many times as I did. I told you this story to show how spirituality operates. Until you master a problem, you are doomed to repeat it. History need not repeat itself if we take a different approach to a problem. The third world war need not happen. WTP are becoming worldwide. WTP of NATO will stand up against the aggression.

Narcissist Infection

Narcissists are like an infection. It spreads if not treated. A narcissist will trash-talk everything. My mother-in-law trash-talked me. Those who choose to follow a narcissist will become infected from the lies. They will become loyal followers, and nothing will change their minds. Even when the lies are obvious, the followers will defend their leader. The followers will gladly trash-talk everyone and everything. They have yet to see the showdown when loyalty makes them betray themselves.

The second thing the followers will do is sink to their leader's level. New lies will be told to get the rush of the drama again. That rush is like a drug. There was no problem in the pizza parlor. Tylor Swift is not part of some conspiracy. Taylor Swift is just a good person. Those caught on the web of the narcissist need to check themselves. They need to wake up. Yes, this is a reference to being woke.

WTP are not good at just following. We can see through the lies and drama.

_____

_____

PART IV

Spirituality

The Flow

I really did not want to explain spirituality. Spirituality cannot be explained. Spirituality must be lived. You are living your own life, and then things happen, and you are in the flow. After getting used to spirituality, you will recognize that you are being called to act with your faith in God.

The flow will bring you good things. The flow will also bring you challenges. Spirituality is about stepping up and learning.

_____

_____

Pass the Test

Will you pass the test? Will you stand up for what is right, or will you remain loyal to the outdated religion or political party? Sin is when you act against what your faith has taught. A sin is a mistake that you keep making. Will you learn and do better?

This time, before you reply in the area below, think long and hard. On the micro (small) level, it is about your life. On the macro (big) level, it is about the government. On the micro level, it is about deciding if you want people to shoot others to satisfy their anger. On the macro level, it is about sensible gun laws.

WTP will act.

_____

_____

Coincidences

Coincidences are another tool of spirituality. Coincidences are like a mini flow. Coincidences are planned in spirit to help you. More times than I can count, I have felt the wind at my back, with things happening at just the right time. It feels like a turn signal that sets me on the right path. It is God, spirit, angels, guides, or whatever you want to call it, and the event helps you.

Wow. I just had another wow moment. I did not think to put this section in. I was all set to write about religion. Then the flow happened, and the appropriate sections took place. Wow.

_____

_____

Thing Happen for a Reason

Most of the time, our lives are uneventful. Other times, there is a reason for what happens. We may not know the reason until after, when we see why it happened. For a good part of my life, I bemoaned the fact that there were so many narcissists in my life. I cried to the heavens to make it stop. I did eventually learn not to be drawn into a relationship with a narcissist. I learned to recognize the red flags and then chose not to be friendly with them.

As you grow older, you do grow smarter. Life will teach you the lessons you need to learn. What repetitive mistakes have you made? Are you tired of it? So, do you want to wake up (woke)?

_____

_____

Aftereffects

After a coincidence, I feel grateful. After a flow, I feel ecstasy. This brings up the Eastern faiths. The map of the chakras was redrawn in the first book, *Confessions from the Closet*. In the East, it is said nothing is ever new, just lost for a while. The eighth through the twelfth chakras are not new. We already own all of them. We have yet to open all of them. Meditation is the key to opening them.

Many people have told me stories about how they, too, have experienced the unexplainable. There are breakthrough events for important events. We do own all the chakras.

I want to say how important the Eastern faiths are. I am well versed in the Western faiths, so I work with them mostly. I am also amazed by the Eastern faiths. Both the Eastern and the Western faiths need to rid themselves of the problems. Both can then progress to spirituality.

The Base

The East and the West both have a problem: corrupt leaders. It's not only political leaders but also religious leaders. Many wars in the past had a particular faith at their root. There are those who have betrayed or forgotten their faith.

The Palestinians and the Jews are the latest example. Both are right, and both are wrong. The faithful are right to follow their faith. The troublemakers misinterpret their faith and are wrong. Aggression is not a part of any faith. There are examples of the mistaken aggression in most faiths. Aggression is only one of the reasons that religions need an upgrade.

WTP inside the different faiths do not live with a hateful heart. The different religions seek love and, in the East, progression. This simply means a better way of living.

The reason I had such a hard time leaving a faith is I truly believe in the wonderful gifts of each faith. Everything has a dark side. This is another spiritual teaching. The trick is to recognize this and be a part of WTP who seek a better world.

_____

_____

Do the Two-Step

There are many steps in spirituality. It involves gradual growing. There are two steps you will repeat on your journey: question and think. Do not be an easy target for someone or something to lead you astray. Question and think about everyone and everything. Think about things that no longer hold true. Then ask yourself what the next step is. Doing the two-step dance is better than just going around in circles, making the same mistake repeatedly.

Epiphanies come to you when you think about just the right thing. Epiphanies are like my wow moments. It is like the sun suddenly comes out, and you are in the light again. Have you ever felt the energy of an epiphany?

_____

_____

School Spirit

Spirit is the nonphysical part of you. Some people call it your soul. Spirit is the what connects us to others and God. It is like when you were in high school or college. You are getting ready for the big football game. Everyone is joined together in fun, tailgating and painting faces and wearing green. Sorry for that; I live in Spartan land. The people on the stands are all connected as one. That is spirit.

School spirit can be a lot of fun. Spiritual spirit allows you to connect to others who are not part of the same team. The twelfth chakra is about understanding. You understand another instead of condemning them. You can finally forgive because you understand the different flaws that made such things possible. You can then work on diminishing the fatal flaws that made it possible. You can speak up against the problem.

Guides and Teachers

Guides are a big factor in spirituality. A guide will help you find your way. You will find a guide who knows the lay of the land of the place you want to go. My guide, My Old Man, was not a passing guide. He was more like a parent that guides a child to reach their potential. I think, in the end, My Old Man was not a guide. He was a tutor, molding me into the adult I became. The many teachers in my closet taught other lessons to me and others. It was a group-learning environment, much like college.

Do not name your guides or teachers. Names are a distraction. Guides and teachers are not meant to be your friends.

_____

_____

The Children

It is true that the younger people will have it easier. The reason for this is they are standing on the backs of those who came before them, both in living well and being well. There is still much work for the youth to do. It will take time for the youth to grow into maturity and understanding. I willingly pass the baton to them. I hope they will bring us all further along. May the children's children keep up the spirit.

I have seen so many large steps forward. I wish I could stick around the next hundred years to see what will be accomplished.

_____

_____

Stay and Remain

Not all people will change. I was born with a few missions to work on. One of the themes was spirituality. I still worked on brain chemistry and addiction. I also worked on family. I did not work on cooking and singing. I know and appreciate those who did work on those things. I love going to concerts and listening to music. I also love going out to eat because I really cannot cook. There are many things that make a well-rounded society.

Getting back to the roots of the faith will keep it pure. Getting back to the roots of the country will keep it safe for all. WTP will keep all safe. WTP will stand against the rotten leaders.

_____

_____

Centered Self

The people who have not stayed true to their roots are self-centered. They think of only what they want. A centered self will see what is best for the country and the world. The divisions within different religions and the fighting among them show that religions are not doing their job. The different countries that go to war for territories are part of the old ways, which will be extinguished when we learn to live in peace. The hippies, the woke, and the WTP can make it so.

Let it be.

_____

_____

PART V

Religions

Expiration Date

With all due respect to the different religions, they are past their expiration dates. Over the many years, religions have done much to make this world a better place. Each religion was formed by a leader for a certain place in time—not for a place but a place in time. Each leader had spiritual gifts. The step up in psychic and spiritual gifts made the leader different, someone who had accomplished what many had never accomplished before. The leaders were, most importantly, teachers and good examples. The leaders were also seen as evil because they came to change things.

Every book, even the Bible (the good book), was written for a certain place and time. I earned a degree in computer sciences in the seventies. The books of that time have little to do with computers now. The same is true with the outdated books of many faiths. The Bible has three parts, the Old Testament, the New Testament, and the Living Testament. Spirituality is the third act of a play where you are responsible for becoming a better person. The New Testament replaced the outdated Old Testament. The Living Testament will replace the New Testament.

There were two most important lessons laid out in the closet with the first book: the chakras and "there is more; there is always more." The next set of chakras shows us how to progress. We have plateaued on the love chakra for far too long. The love chakra also holds all emotions, including hate and anger. We need to move on. There will be more. There will always be more.

_____

_____

Changing Times

Yes, the times are changing. Time has changed us. In days gone by, only a few could work with spirit. Spiritual abilities are becoming more common. WTP have evolved to the next level. No longer do we need a leader in government or in religion.

Many times, when I spoke about my first book, people would confide in me that they too had experienced the extra knowing. What story do you have to tell when you too had an experience?

_____

_____

Do Not Like Change

Many of us do not like change. I have seen so many changes in my life. Over time, I grew to be grateful for the changes. Just think of it. I got a black-and-white TV with three channels. When I first started writing, I had to type and type, and corrections were pointless. Now, with the computer, writing is so much easier. Later, we will all be grateful for the changes that are about to happen.

When I was young, I remember being amazed when the family went to visit our uncle who had bought the first color TV. I knew then and there that I would welcome changes. Change was no longer something to fear. Please be excited about the coming changes.

_____

_____

Leaving Religions

Religions too will change with the new era. WTP do not follow a leader anymore. The reason for this is that we have grown or learned enough; we no longer need to follow. WTP no longer need an intermediary between us and God. We still need to work on ourselves to become the best version of ourselves. This is what spirituality is for.

Being your best self is the inevitable next step. Do you dare take up the challenge and leave the safety of the old religions behind?

Religions Will Fade Away

Even now, there is a decline in membership in most religions. It is time to pass the baton for the next step. Spirituality is like WTP. There is no leader to follow. Each person is growing into the private connection to God, or spirit, or all, or many other names. In spirituality, there is no need to quibble over a certain name or idea or method.

Namaste. The god in me sees the god in you. The different religions are no more than different languages saying the same thing. A rose by any other name is still a rose. God, by any other name, is still God.

Each meeting with the team began and ended the same way. They would nod their heads and say, "Greetings," to start or, "All for now" to end. Meeting with the team is different from going to the school. I am no longer in class; I am a coworker. I have grown enough to become a teammate. Will you grow?

_____

_____

The Problem with Religions

The problem is that when anything is past the expiration date, things begin to rot and stink. We can all see the blatant rot. It would be hard to innumerate all the troublemakers we can see. Some of the troublemakers take cover behind their religion and are blind to the trouble they make. They are blindly following a faith that has been and is being misinterpreted by a leader.

A spiritual lesson is that everything has a dark side. Twisting a good thing to their own agenda, the stinky leader will trash-talk anyone not of their tribe. The rotten leader will declare a war on anyone not following them.

I made it without the team pointing a finger at me. I got close to judging people and complaining about them. I am learning.

_____

_____

Way It Was, Not as It Will Be

We are living on the crux of a new age. So many things will change. COVID took the lives of many people. Many more will pass as climate change forces a change on the planet. There are indeed hard times ahead. WTP can make a choice to embrace it all and work to live in different times, or we can complain and ignore what we see happening.

Sometimes it never occurs to us that we have a choice.

_____

_____

A Bad Example

If I cannot be a good example, let me be a horrible reminder. My late husband is a horrible reminder. He was a man. He did not want to show weakness. He kept quiet about what he was feeling. (As I write this now, a cardinal is on a tree branch in front of me. Just another spiritual thing.) His coughing was getting worse.

He was having problems eating. Food would get stuck in his throat, and he would cough until it went down. Eventually, it was so bad that he would excuse himself and go to the restroom. I forced him to go to a doctor, but it was too late. Esophageal cancer took his life.

I could not change my husband. The choice was his. In facing the future, the choice is ours. When you make a choice, think of others too.

_____

_____

In the Beginning

There are many religions on this planet. Each religion has its value. Each religion has its own idea about how to live life. Every religion speaks about God. That one thing they all have in common is important. The different religions are no more than different languages saying the same thing. A rose by any other name is still a rose. God, by any other name, is still God.

I cannot understand why the Jews are hated. I cannot understand why the Catholics and the Protestants fought for years in England. I cannot understand people of faith who hold hate in their hearts.

_____

_____

PART VI

People Change

New Styles

For those of you who are afraid to change, think of it as a new style. You do not want to wear clothes that are out of style. Each generation will have its own imprint on style.

The Nehru jacket will never return, but I did own one. It expired. You really would not be caught dead in a leisure suit anymore. I did not own one. One thing I did like about being a hippie is you could wear a mini a maxi or any length skirt. We were more accepting of differences. The hippies did not even care what color you were. We were ahead of our time. We were the seed of WTP.

_____

_____

Religion Can Stay

Many parts of the world will remain as we have always known them. Even the physical aspects of the change will still have parts that remain the same. There will also be new lands. There are those who will not leave their faiths. There are those who follow the root of their faith and are very spiritual. There is no need to change if you are already doing spiritual work.

Hippies did not care what faith you were. The hippie faith was basically peace and love. If you want to keep your ways, that is cool. Right on. Never underestimate us old hippies.

Plateaued

Everything will change. Everything is always changing. Think of the old religions as plateauing. Plateauing is staying in one place too long. I know all about this. When you are on a diet, you stay the same for a while until your body adjusts, and then you can move on again.

My team first taught that staying on the heart chakra is just plateauing. There is more. There is always more.

_____

_____

Religious Leaders

Again, not all leaders are corrupt. It is the few bad apples who are making even their followers rotten. WTP of all faiths have remained silent too long. Remaining a good member in standing is more important to some than standing up for what is right. This goes for membership in both a faith and a given political party.

I am happy knowing I am not a leader. When I was a Girl Scout leader, I wore a baseball cap that said, "Don't follow me, I am lost," as a stream of girls walked behind me.

_____

_____

Do Not Feel Bad

If you are a little put off or offended as I speak about the old faiths, think about how I felt when I was called a devil for many years because of psychic vision. Think about how the blacks felt as they were vilified for so many years. Think about how many gays were killed for simply existing. Karma can be good if you do good. Karma can be bad if you do harm. Learn your lesson and move on. You will not be punished. God is not like that. God was a punishing God when we were still young in understanding.

Just like with our parents; they would often punish us when we were young. Now, as an adult, I can have a different relationship with my parents. WTP have grown enough to know God as a loving God. You will only resolve to do better and become better.

_____

_____

Science

Science has not always been right either. Science thought the Earth was flat. Then we learned more and understood more. We once thought the Earth was the center of the solar system. Then we learned more and understood more. Science has made mistakes and then advanced past the old ideas. It was not easy for science to do this. It is not easy to accept a change in what is collectively accepted.

Science could accept it was time to change. Will the people of faith also see that it is time to change?

WTP and Choice

WTP have reached a point where we can no longer blindly follow. In times gone by, people were happy to follow a leader. The people were not yet ready for the responsibility of running things. The leaders of old were trained to take care of things. There was a generational aspect to leaders. The future leaders were trained to run the country by those who came before them.

The expiration date for the old-school leaders had not yet come. Slowly, the commoners learned enough to take control. Their time was coming. WTP progressed enough to realize all that was needed to keep things moving along. Democracies were taking their turn leading. Sadly, it was only the rich who made all the rules. The idea of equality had yet to be realized. Slowly, equality started to seep in. Women won the right to vote. Women began to have a voice and speak out. Following that was the realization that the leaders could no longer lead. The black and the brown demanded equality. LGBTQ no longer hid in the closet. They demanded a right to be.

I have seen so many changes in my years. There is a quickening in progress. There is a widening in progress. I know many do not think change was fast enough. I know it takes the time it takes. I know the pace is picking up for the new age.

Freedom

This country has fought for freedom many times—freedom from those who want to rule over us. The fight for freedom has turned into the right of freedom. The old religions will remain. That is their right. The females will not be ruled over. Freedom is their right. Once freedom has been tasted, it cannot be taken away. The LGBTQ too are now grateful for living in the land of freedom.

This country was founded on the idea of freedom from those who wanted to rule over us. The creeps are now something that must be dealt with. The creeps who are coming out from under the rocks are many. Exposure to the light is the best disinfectant. The sun itself has UV rays that destroy bacteria. Shining a light and exposing the lies and motives of the creeps is the answer.

WTP know that we will stand for freedom. WTP will stand up for freedom—freedom for all.

In my school in the sky, there was another important lesson. Everyone gets a turn at bat. WTP do not want the last batter to take a swing at things again. They had their turn. WTP do not want the old ideas from Europe, with just one religion to lead the country. They have had their turn.

_____

_____

New Age, New Ways

Times have changed. Eras have changed. The upcoming changes need WTP to work together to handle the challenges. WTP means all the people. WTP means equality. There is no need to fight for superiority among us. Stepping back into the old-school ways will only bring harm. WTP will have heroes, and people will band together to face all three challenges that are bringing the new age. COVID, climate change, and creeps (CCC) must be dealt with. WTP can figure out ways to overcome anything.

I really cannot think of anything to add to this. The future will be what we make it.

_____

_____

Change Comes in Stages

Change is not an overnight thing. Change takes decades to really start. It is like a seed that is planted. Years will pass before it is a tree. Each year, bit by bit, it grows. I was part of the hippie generation that wanted to give peace a chance. I know we are now threatened by another world war. I also know that there are enough WTP who are working for peace. Change is going to come.

I can feel it. I can see it. COVID, climate change, and the creeps are forcing us to accept the changes.

_____

_____

Explorer, Pioneer, Civilization

WTP are seeking an evolution and not a revolution. Revolution just ends with another poor leader in charge. Evolution takes time. I do consider myself an explorer. I did not know much about all the psychic/ spiritual things that were thrust upon me. I was simply born that way. My grandmother was the closest thing to a teacher that I had. She left me at a very early age. I was a quiet child who was good at observing. I explored all the different things I could do that I knew others could not.

The pioneers in the psychic fields were just coming into their own. I suddenly knew I was not alone. There were others like me, and we would eventually grow in number. We collectively claimed our place in this land. I see the same thing happening with the blacks and the browns and the LBGTQs. The pioneers in each of these fields laid down the groundwork that was needed. All of them were the first heroes of WTP.

Then came a civilization that had collectively progressed. It took time to mature and grow. But look at us now.

I was just told to add one more important ingredient: education. After World War II, the general population went into higher education. The commoners were now being trained to be leaders and doers. The stage was then set for WTP.

Next Step

When the printing press made books more accessible, knowledge became more common. Humankind started a growth spurt. When the internet came along, another growth spurt took place. Researching the different subjects helped people learn new things. You just had to hit a few keys instead of looking for a book and then reading it. The internet made learning like getting the CliffsNotes. For the younger people, CliffsNotes is a summary of a whole book.

Short, little, bite-size ideas are the way the team works with me. The same method is displayed in the books we write. It just makes learning easier. It is about teaching, not preaching.

_____

_____

PART VII

UFOs

It Is *Not* What It Was

Yes, the government has been covering up the truth about UFOs. The government has recently become open about UFOs. This was a baby step. Change takes time, and the changing times are forcing the acceptance of UFOs. The government became open because they knew UFOs were also coming out of the closet to help with CCC.

We are on the brink of another world war. WTP are working to stop it. UFOs will stop it. UFOs are being seen more now because they are watching out for us.

I have never seen a UFO. I have always wanted to live long enough to see one. I knew the time was coming.

_____

_____

UFOs Were Denied

In the forties, the denial started. The world was not ready to accept UFOs. Had UFOs been acknowledged, it would have upended the foundations of the country and even the world. The faiths of the world could never accept what believing in UFOs meant. Belief in the UFOs would mean denial of the foundations of the different religions. The times have changed. Now, we must change.

This is just one more example of outdated concepts. The seed of accepting UFOs was planted a few generations ago. WTP will accept UFOs. Well, at least this WTP will.

_____

_____

Look Past the Past

Part of looking to the future includes putting the past in the past. The time has come to admit the UFOs are real. This is a big change. Accepting UFOs also means knowing that the past ways are expiring.

Spirituality addresses this with the concept of time and space. Spirituality also addresses the concept of the soul and God. Spirituality includes what I have known all my life. I have been a psychic since birth. Whenever I faced a big problem in my life, I learned and then grew spiritually. The same will be true as WTP see the need to grow because of the changes that are coming.

The faiths of old are no longer good enough. I am tired of all the wars fought and still being fought because of religious beliefs. There is more. There is always more.

_____

_____

UFOs and the Atom Bomb

UFOs will be taking part in the new era. UFOs are aware of the changes to come, and many of them want to help. The biggest help will be stopping the old school from using the atom bomb. Once exposed in this manner, WTP will expand to the stars. The citizens of Earth will then be citizens of the stars.

This too is a yet to be. I do suggest that you get ready for it. For now, it is enough to know that UFOs are real.

I always wanted to live long enough to see UFOs. I might live long enough. I might not. Will I get my wish?

_____

_____

Webb Telescope

We are not alone. The exploration of space with the telescopes has opened our eyes to how big the universe is. The universe is overflowing with planets and suns and worlds. The biblical concept of how the world was created is just too small to be real. God is bigger than just this one world.

There is a reason I kept the UFOs for the end. There is enough resistance to religious acceptance and change. Accepting UFOs is a whole other thing. The Webb pictures are amazing.

_____

_____

ETs in History

History, deep history, shows that others from other planets have been here before. The mythology of the ancient Greeks, with their warring and ruling gods, was not just a religion. It was a fact. Deeper civilizations made a leap with the help of beings from other planets. The missing link was the intervention of other beings.

It was a sort of gene therapy that improved the beings of that time.

ETs' First Purpose

It has been said that the ETs wanted to create a slave race to mine the riches of Earth. That is true. The people of Earth had yet to evolve into a higher consciousness. The people were happy to simply follow their leader. In ancient history, the leader was often a hybrid. There is a reason the ruling class wanted to keep the genes of their family strong.

This lingering thought is why the white race thinks it needs to be pure. This is an outdated, needless belief. It is too late. The genes are already with everyone to some degree.

Time Changes Things

It is not a fault that the early people were such good followers. The people of that time needed to marinate long enough to become more distinct. Little by little, the people matured. The people of that time matured enough to be unmanageable to the rulers. Time was up. They left. There is more. There is always more.

The different eras had different ways of being. Progress is slow. We even backslide at times. WTP will not backslide.

_____

_____

ETs and Hybrids

There is some validity to spiritual gifts being strong in some families. Even the virgin birth had many prior similar events in history. It is said that the visiting being slept with females to create a hybrid. The hybrid had many talents given to it by the "father." Rome, Egypt, China, and the Bible had virgin births.

That is just from recorded history. There is more. There is always more.

ETs' Impregnations

Even the Bible has hints of UFOs. The burning bush was a craft. The Ark of the Covenant was built from instructions for how to create it. Who told them? Who gave the instructions for how to build the ark? I do not want to discredit the Bible. The Bible was written for the eyes of another time. They could not understand things yet because they had not yet developed enough. Some man in the past said being gay was an abomination, so the Christians adhere to that. In that time, they knew no better. Abortion was also nothing new. All recorded times have had people who were gay. I could go on, but you see the point of questioning the roots of your faith.

_____

_____

Virgin Births

It is said that the visiting being slept with females to create a hybrid. The science of the visitors knew the process of birth. It had nothing to do with beauty. Many faiths thought it was because the females were so pretty, they could not resist them. This resulted in keeping the females under wraps and hidden. Prior to those days, females could even be rulers, as in the Egyptian nation. The Eastern faiths hold to the memory of hiding wemen. It has no place in this era.

Keeping females hidden made them second-class citizens. They could no longer grow and learn. The idea of the two genders not being equal is another thing that needs to be erased from the collective consciousness. Did you know that what you think is just an imprint from the collective consciousness? We are all free to exit that kind of thinking.

_____

_____

Each Country Had a Religion

Each country going back in time had a belief system. Each country had its own connection to whatever their concept of God was. The Native Americans had their shamans. Ancient Egypt had their faith leadership established by a group of gods. This religion included the belief in an afterlife and the elaborate steps needed to get to the afterlife. The ancient Greeks had many gods to worship. The Greeks gods were a family of gods. Each god had its own area to oversee.

It is true that many of the ancient leaders were hybrids.

_____

_____

Different Parts of Faith

Each religion has the concept of separating the jobs needed in a faith. The faith of my family was Catholicism, so I learned to pray to certain saints for certain things. St. Anthony was the saint of fertility. In ancient Egypt, Ocyurus oversaw fertility. He could influence the birth of a son in which to live again. Even the wiccan had their deities to pray to for help. Egypt had many gods that were pictured merging with man and animals. Later, the gods were no longer there, and the pharaohs ran the country. Thus, a generational ruling class was born.

History has much to teach us. A partial history will not teach us. UFOs are real.

Real-Life Example

This is how coincidences happen. Yesterday, I posted on Facebook that I was having a pity party.

I only had one person come to my party. This morning when I woke up and went to the computer, there was an unusual post. It was one of those look-back-on-your-memories posts. There was a picture of my daughter. This was the first time an older picture came up. She was killed in a car accident more than twenty years ago. I do not know how it happened. I do not care. She came to comfort me.

First Act

The map my teachers use for the chakras is different. The magic board behind the teacher illustrates what the lesson is. This lesson started with a triangle. The first three chakras create the triangle. Updating the idea of yin as feminine and yang as masculine. We now can use extrovert and introvert. The last element of the triangle is not the base, it is the brains of the operation.

The double named chakras are important in the new map. These chakras are two distinct chakras. The root and the base do different jobs. The sacral and the navel could not be more different. The third eye and the brow are different. Ben, my eastern teacher, reminds me that the east believes nothing is new, just forgotten for a while.

The first three chakras combine to start off the being you are to be. The base chakra along with the sacral and solar plexus chakras create the sides of the triangle. The team looks at the sets of chakras and what their job is. The three work together. The sacral is the energy or extrovert quality. The solar plexus is the figuring things out or the brains of the operation. The base has an introvertive quality.

Over many years the three chakras work together to create the matrix of the being. The child creates an identity. It is a mistake to think that the ego is the same as an identity. The ego is a sense of importance. The child's identity is tied up with growing up. The child thinks everything is "mine". The identity does not yet include others.

At some point the child hears the calling of others. The child exits its ego to become part of something bigger. The child is influenced by the heart chakra to become part of a family. The small triangle becomes a part of the larger triangle of the next set of chakras.

Spirituality teaches that there is a dark side to everything. Mistakes are made. On the micro(small) level, if the child does not exit its idea of the ego that tells him he is important, the child becomes a narcissist. A narcissist creates chaos to get attention and to get its way in everything. It is the dark side.

On the macro (large) level the same scenario is played out with countries and different groups. The dark side of religions can be seen here. The KKK warped the faith to create chaos to forward its own ideas. Hamas warped the faith of the fathers to create chaos. Even today, the right in America is forcing itself on others. It is not just the groups within the countries that are a problem. It can be the countries themselves that are a problem. Israel still is nursing a wound and will not realize that others are calling out to them to exit their personal ego and join others in peace. Russa thinks of itself as being so grand that everything is "mine".

Second Act

The next three chakras create the second act of your life. The three contributors for the next triangle are the crown, the throat, and the third eye. The heart called to you. The heart is all about feelings. The extravert of the throat is you communicating with others. The introvertive eyes take things in as you work on growing relationships. The crowning glory is figuring out your life and purpose. The second act is much longer than the first act.

It will take years to learn about relationships. The second triangle is five times bigger than the first triangle. It is a mistake to think the heart chakra is all about love. There is a dark side to the heart too. The heart holds all feelings. Love and hate. Passion and anger.

We accumulate many feelings as we grow. Feelings are a wonderful teacher. The feelings of love and even the feeling of liking someone help us to get along with others. We, as a being, come to earth to work on certain things. The introvert in you will see things that you like. We will be attracted to the things we like. Like a bee to a flower, you will gravitate towards your purpose.

The negative feelings are not all bad. The negative feelings will keep you safe. Hurting is a great teacher also. When something hurts you, you should learn not to do the same thing again. Sometimes it will take two or three times to get hurt before you learn. Sometimes you will never learn the lesson.

I, the writer, learned this with narcissists. Learning took a few tries. Later in life, when living made me wiser, I learned a better way. One of my greatest tools is that I am a helpful person. I like to get along with people. This is both a blessing and a curse. A narcissist will be attracted to you like a bee to a flower. I had to learn that NO is not always negative. I had to learn to not step into the trap. I have seen a few narcissists since I learned the lesson. My first inclination is to help people. Narcissists are like wolves in sheep's clothing, I began to recognize a person that only takes and never gives. I learned.

Addiction is another thing that keeps hurting you. You do not even realize that you are being hurt because you only feel the good of being high. Discernment is needed to escape the trap. Discernment is being able to truly see a problem and not just feel. The third eye allows you to look deep into things. The third eye is more than just seeing. This special eye is like a brain as it connects what you are seeing with what has happened before. The brain also figures things out and an addict knows on some level that it is a problem, but the addict does not see a way out.

I have seen three different ways to escape the trap of addiction. My husband went to NA. The book, *A Course in Miracles* was channeled by a person that cried out for a better way. I, the writer, see things in colors. NA and *A Course in Miracles* carry the same color. The third person to escape told me how she was sick and tired of being sick and tired and returned to the roots of her faith. The problem for this person was men. They learned.

Third Act

The next calling will be the forgotten next step. It is your birthright to own all the chakras. The eighth chakra has had breakthrough events that let you know there is more. Most people will experience a psychic event a few times in their lives. Others have been experiencing it all their lives. The question is, how do you find what you have forgotten?

Meditation. The spiritual gifts were not for the general population in the past. People had to choose to enter a monastery to devote themselves the seeking of spirit and God. Seeking is much easier now with the internet. We no longer need to solely seek God. When you enter the flow, that feeling of the wind at your back that shows you are headed in the right direction, you feel like God is seeking you.

Meditation will wake up the next chakra. The eighth chakra is at the back and base of the skull. Every chakra's birthplace is in a gland. Meditation affects the carotid gland. The carotid gland is found to be larger in the autopsies of people that meditate regularly. Meditation is all about breathing. The breathing affects the amount of oxygen in the blood. Not much is known about the substance secreted from this gland. I am not surprised by this.

The double names chakras are partners with the eighth chakra. The root and the navel and the brow complete the triangle. Because the eighth chakra is in the back, it changes the direction of the triangles. The triangle is pointing down this time. Superimposing the new chakra on the triangle started by the heart creates the star of David. I am not surprised by this either.

I found the eighth chakra, so I got to name it. I call it the unity chakra. We begin to feel like we are connected to everything. The unity chakra is the reason reading can be done. The navel chakra is the connection to God. The navel is the reason healing can be done. The root chakra connects you to the Earth realm. The root is the reason we can remember lives gone by. The brow chakra will figure things out. There is so much to figure out at this point.

It is important to note here that lives gone by are not personally your past life. Returning to the Earth realm is about incarnation not reincarnation. When I flew on trips with my husband, I was surprised by seeing that the trees had a shadow. Is it the shadow or the shade of the tree? The famous picture of the vase, that when viewed differently, becomes two people looking at each other. When you change your focus, you see things differently.

The opening of the unity chakra is easier than you think. Meditation is all about the breathing. The early meditation practices teach you to slow down and calm down. The Earth realm is such a busy place. The spirit realm is slow and peaceful. Basically, the two are incompatible. Meditation is the bridge between the two. By the time you are ready for the unity chakra, you have learned the value of slowing down. You can breathe in and slowly count to four. You can hold your breath for the count of four. You can slowly breathe out for the count of four. I like to do this when I am at a red light. The slower breathing will continue as you drive. No need to count. You only needed to slow down while breathing. I feel the relaxation as I drive on. Eventually the unity chakra will awaken.

Furthermore

Next, yes there is a next. There is a calling of the twelfth chakra. This one really blew my mind. The triangles multiplied until it was like the Merkabah star and a lotus blossom. I am not surprised by this either. All for now.

Printed in the United States
by Baker & Taylor Publisher Services